YOU CAN COME IN ANYWAY

By Reid Brockway

Illustrations by Susan Brockway

YOU CAN COME IN ANYWAY

First written and illustrated around 1990.
Poetry by Reid Brockway. Illustrations by Susan Brockway.

Copyright © 2021 by Reid and Susan Brockway
Seattle, Washington USA
Do not reproduce in any form

Library of Congress Control Number: 2021911150

ISBN: 978-1-7373167-0-1

FOREWARD

My dad wrote this book of poetry. He made me learn and recite "How to Skin an Elephant" for my second-grade class. He also made me learn pi backwards from the sixteenth place past the decimal point as a party trick for his friends. Surprisingly, I still remember it, and the aforementioned poem.

Dad's jokes, puns and poems have always made me groan; groan in a way that though, despite having heard some of them over and over again, I sort of like. I even tell my friends now and then that if at first they don't succeed they should just "suck something else". Yes, it's rubbed off. Oops.

Mom's artwork is delicate, detailed, and full of life. She is his muse and heartbeat. She's also his co-conspirator, though she won't want to admit it.

I'm proud of their effort.

~ CJ Brockway, daughter

CONTENTS

INTRODUCTION

FREEDOM	1
THE INVENTOR OF LINT	2
SALLY AND THE SALAD BAR	4
THE REPAIRMAN	10
NOTHING TO DO	12
THE GARBAGE GUT	14
BLIMP PARKING	16
THE MONSTERS ARE OUT TONIGHT	22
ABOUT FROGS	26
SEXY?	30
TEN TONS OF TURKEY TOES	32
ON BEING A BIRD	38
MULTIPLICATION	40
FISH STORY	44
A MAGIC SPELL, OR SOMETHING	48
STRANGE THINGS TO EAT	50
A TUBE FULL OF PEOPLE	52
GROWNUPS FOR GROWNUPS	56
IF I COULD DRIVE A CAR	58
GOOD ADVICE	62
HOW TO SKIN AN ELEPHANT	64
FORTS	66
PRETTY CLEVER FOR A RABBIT	70
THE FIRST TIME	80
MY FAVORITE TREE	82
THE DRUMMER	84
WHAT DO ANIMALS THINK	86
THE DATE	88
I WANT TO BE A GARBAGE MAN	90
USED CANDY	91
TOYS	93
LOLLIPOPS AND LEARNING TO FLY	94
SOMETHING LEFT TO DO	98
LIFE IN A DUNGEON	102
THE MARCHING BAND	104
THE KID WHO LIVES UPSTAIRS	108

INTRODUCTION

This is a children's book. Well, not exactly. It's a children's book for adults ...*and* kids. Especially adult kids - those of us who, though grown up, still have a playful streak and the capacity to view the world through the eyes of a child.

The themes in this book are youthful. The poems feature kids or are told by kids. But there is an undercurrent of adult humor or insight in all of them. They are designed to be read to and entertain children, yet at the same time amuse the grownup reader. And as the child matures, maybe reading the poems on their own, they will come to appreciate both levels themselves (maybe surprisingly soon!).

There is also a touch of political incorrectness in some of these poems. Kids do **not** go out and shoot elephants, of course, so instructions on how to skin an elephant are clearly whimsical. And it can be frightening for a small child to think about suddenly turning into a rabbit and having to figure out how to communicate with their parents. This is where the adult has a role to play, assuring the child that "This is just pretend" or noting "What a silly idea!", perhaps saving a few of these until the child is a bit older. But in the end, being able to appreciate and laugh at something that is slightly off-color is part of growing up.

Finally, this book can be a springboard for discussion. Would anyone really have to *invent* lint? Why *do* dandelions make so many seeds? And who is "the kid who lives upstairs"? When the time is right, the adult and child can meet on the same level.

Meanwhile, this is a book meant for children, but you can come in anyway.

FREEDOM

Fun things to do
Nothing to do

Want to get up
Don't have to get up

Sunny all day
Lazy ol' day

Best time of year
Summer is here

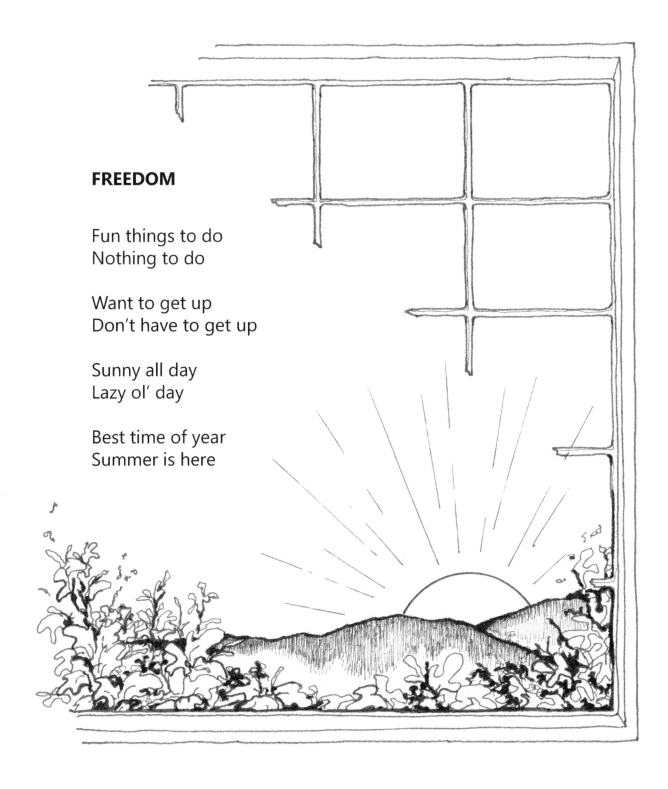

THE INVENTOR OF LINT

Did you ever wonder where lint comes from?
Why, just about anywhere you can find some,
Like inside your pockets and stuck to dark clothes,
In your belly button... (achoo!) and your nose.

But I'll bet you haven't so much as a hint
That Finklestein was the *inventor* of lint.
An insect collector, he struggled to stuff
The bugs he was stuffing with cottonseed fluff.

Then he made up his mind what the world needed was
Some new kind of stuffing, some kind of a fuzz
Much smaller than cotton or goose down by far,
To stuff in the tiniest places there are.

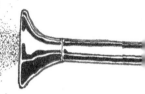

So he built a machine that would eat up old blankets,
Seat cushions, old sox... stuff like that, when he'd crank it;
And out would come lint just as fine as you please
That shifted and drifted about in the breeze.

"I'll package it," Finklestein thought, "and I'll sell it.
The world will go crazy for lint when I tell it!"
So he took it to stores and to big companies
And advertised with moneyback guarantees.

But no one would buy it, not even his friends.
And that's where the story of lint almost ends.
Yet still there's no shortage of lint, for you see,
Ever since he's been cranking the stuff out for free.

SALLY AND THE SALAD BAR

Little Sally Sullivan
Was smaller than most small kids are,
But little Sally Sullivan
Just loved to eat from a salad bar.

    Now, you may wonder what being small
    Could have to do with lettuce and all.
    Well Sally, you see, had to stand on a chair
    To see what salad stuff was there.

And once when she went out to dine
Where the salad bar was especially fine,
With monstrous bowls of this and that
All sunk in ice, in a leafy mat,

    Poor Sally had a frightful scare;
    For standing there upon a chair
    And reaching for the crouton bin,
    Little Sally... fell in!

She came up first in the spinach greens
And blurted out a tiny scream.
But, before the others knew,
Again poor Sally sank from view.

    She came up next in a giant bowl
    Of seafood salad a'creole
    With shrimp and peppers all around.
    Then with a gasp she went back down.

        She came up in a fruit bowl then
        And next tomato gelatin
        And then a bowl of chopped-up meats
        And after that the pickled beets.

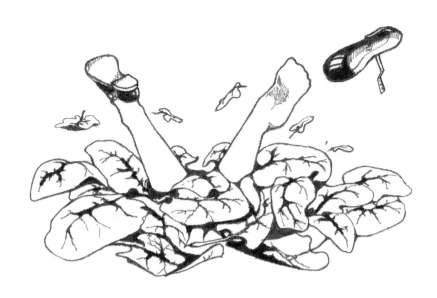

And then when she was almost shot,
She came up in a dressing pot
And grabbed ahold of a breadstick where
Some slob had left it floating there.

    So then when she could finally float
    She caught her breath and cleared her throat;
    And when she gave a frantic shout
    Her fellow diners pulled her out.

Sally's now a better swimmer;
But, when she goes out to dinner,
Though the salad bar's sublime,
It's dinner salads every time.

THE REPAIRMAN

Last night I had an accident
When Mom was visiting next door;
While trying to find where the candy's hid
I knocked her teapot to the floor.

It broke into a bunch of parts,
And I thought I was really had!
But clever me, I thought up how
She won't find out that I was bad.

I fixed the thing myself, you see.
And I know Mom will never know;
'Cause I fixed it with transparent tape
All stuck *inside* where it won't show!

NOTHING TO DO

There's nothing to do today...
Except, of course, to draw a horse,
Or else, perhaps, to run some laps,
Or maybe I could make a pie,
Or if not cook, then read a book.
Although... I *could* explore the woods,
Or else, let's see, go climb a tree;
Or I just might go fly my kite,
Or find some rags and make a flag,
Or draw with chalk on our front walk.
Perhaps I'll play with modeling clay,
Or go outside and sneak and hide.
Maybe I could be a spy,
Or be a rat and tease the cat,
Or toss the ball against the wall,
Or paint my face, or run a race,
Or chase a dog, or catch a frog,
Or take a hike, or ride my bike...

But first, oh gloom! I hafta' clean my room.
There's nothing to do today.

THE GARBAGE GUT

Gerald is a garbage gut;
There's nothing he won't eat.
Each day he goes to lunch with us
And plops down in his seat
And opens up his paper bag
And starts to cram stuff in
And eats it all almost before
The rest of us begin.

The other day we all agreed
It really would be great
To do a secret test to see
If **he knew** what he ate.
We got ahold of Gerald's lunch
And found his roast beef san'
And neatly put inside of it
A bunch of rubber bands.

At lunch that day we all sat there
And tried hard not to smile
As Gerald chomped his sandwich with
His normal piggy style.
He chewed a little more, perhaps,
And worked at swallowing,
But to our surprise, the garbage gut
Wolfed down the whole darn thing!

BLIMP PARKING

Danny McDougal lived on a farm
Right next to the county fair,
And every year when the fair would come
All the action would be right there.
Just over the fence in a great big field
Were the carnival rides and the games;
And Danny would watch all the kids having fun
And say to himself, "It's a shame
I don't have some money so I could go, too,
More than just once or twice.
I need to make money... Some kind of a job...
Something easy and fun would be nice."

Then he got an idea. "I can let them park cars
Right here in my father's field.
A dollar a car. All I do is direct.
I'll be rich! I'll be rich!" he squealed.
But Mr. McDougal was not too impressed
When Danny asked for his consent.
"It'll kill all the grass that the cow needs to eat,
And besides, there's no gate in the fence,
And the oil from the cars will get all over things,
And..."
    "Never mind," Danny sighed.
Then he went off to think of another idea,
But he couldn't, as hard as he tried.

It was on the next day the idea finally came.
As Danny looked up in the air,
A blimp floated by, all lit up with bright lights
Saying COME TO THE COUNTY FAIR.
With a saw from the barn Danny cut off the limbs
From the field's only tree. (It was dead.)
Then he made a big sign, laid it flat on the ground
By the tree. BLIMP PARKING, it said.

"Blimps just *float* there," said Danny.
"OK," said his dad, "but I doubt that you'll get it to park."
Sure enough, Danny waited... and waited... and waited...
and waited... until it was dark,
And again the next day, but the blimp never came,
And Danny was not at all pleased.
And as for his father, he wasn't much help.
More hindrance. "How's business?" he teased.

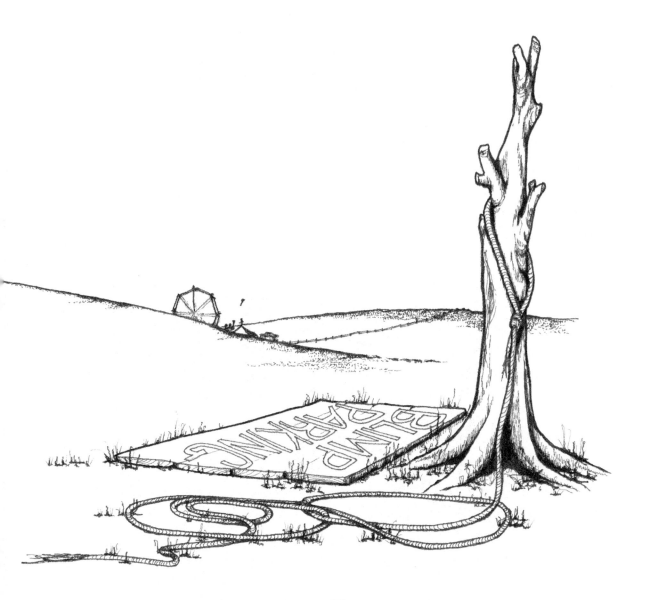

But just two days later Danny came to his dad
And handed him twenty-five bucks.
His dad's eyebrows lifted, he muttered, "What's this?"
And he looked like he'd been thunderstruck.

"It's the money I made from the kids at the fair,"
Said Danny with obvious pride.
"I noticed they needed a good place to put
Their balloons when they went on the rides.
So I redid my sign so it said BALLOON PARKING
And put it right next to the fence.
Kids came by the hundreds! Already I've made
Thirty dollars and sixty-eight cents."

"But why?" asked his father. "But why are you giving
This twenty-five dollars to me?"
"For part of the fence that is missing," said Danny,
His embarrassment easy to see.

"Missing?" his father exclaimed. "Where'd it go?"
And then Danny tipped back his head
And peered at the sky with the funniest look.

"Up," is all that he said.

THE MONSTERS ARE OUT TONIGHT

The monsters are out tonight,
The terrible creatures all ghastly and gross
That jump out and get you if you come too close.
The monsters are out tonight.

It wouldn't be safe outside.
If you and I dared to set foot out the door
They'd probably never see *us* anymore.
It wouldn't be safe outside.

I dare you to come with me.
Although it's not safe out, I'm still gonna go.
I'm not scared of monsters; I trap them, you know.
I dare you to come with me.

You'll do it? OK, let's go.
But be very careful and stay very close.
You don't *have* to do it; I'm braver than most.
You'll do it? OK, let's go.

G-gosh, it's sure dark outside.
It *is* kinda' creepy. Let's stay close to home.
The thing about monsters -- **all over** they roam.
G-gosh, it's sure dark outside.

Let's set up our trap right here.
You hide in those bushes and I'll hide in these.
We'll trip one, then scram while it's down on its knees.
Let's set up our trap right here.

I hear something coming now.
Remember to pull on the rope when I yell.
This is an ugly one, I can just tell.
I hear something coming... NOW!

...oops

Quick, back to the house and hide.
I told you that tripping a beast can go bad.
That isn't a monster, that beast is my dad.
Quick, back to the house and hide.

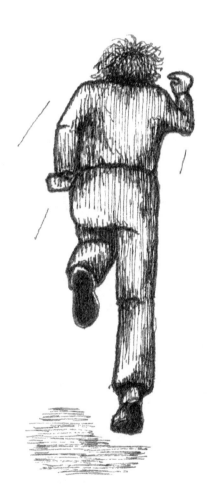

ABOUT FROGS

Frogs make really good pets.
Most folks don't know that.
They think pets should be furry and warm
Like... a dog or cat.

Folks would change their minds
If they only knew --
Frogs have a lotta' advantages.
Here are just a few:

Frogs are well-behaved.
They don't make very much noise.
They don't leave furballs on the carpet
Or chew up clothes or toys.

You don't hafta' get them shots.
Keepin' frogs is free.
You don't buy them flea collars, powder 'n stuff...
Ever heard of a frog with fleas?

For food they just eat bugs,
And catchin' bugs is fun.
And if your frog disappears or "croaks"
You just catch another one.

Parents don't hassle ya 'bout 'em
Like they do for other pets.
If you trade a frog for a toy or somethin'
Your mother won't get upset.

Frogs don't chase the mailman.
They don't get into frog fights.
They don't bug the neighbors or tear up the house,
Or leave you with scratches or bites.

You can keep a frog in your pocket
Or under your hat, on your head.
They make tiny lumps so your mom doesn't know
If you take your pet frog to bed.

Yup, frogs have a lotta' advantages
Over pets of most other sorts.
Of course, there's just one thing I've been wonderin'...
Do you know if they really cause warts?

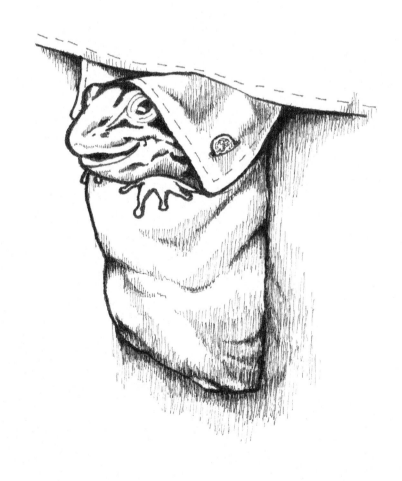

SEXY?

A boy said my sister is sexy.
I'm not 'zactly sure what that means.
I think it has something to do with her hair
Or maybe the style of her jeans.

I tried to get her to explain it,
And she said to wait till I grow.
My mother said it's just too hard to explain,
And my father said he didn't know.

If someone told me that *I'm* sexy
I'm not 'zactly sure what I'd do.
I might get embarrassed or might punch 'em out,
Or might just call **them** sexy, too.

TEN TONS OF TURKEY TOES

What happened while Mommy was taking her nap?

Nothing.

Nobody called on the phone?

No.

Nobody came to the door?

No……….. A man with a great big truck came to the door.

Oh, and did you answer it?

What?

The door!

Uh-huh.

And what did the man say?

He asked if this is the… the… It was numbers.

He asked if he had the right address?

Uh-huh.

And what did you tell him?

Yes.

And what did he say then?

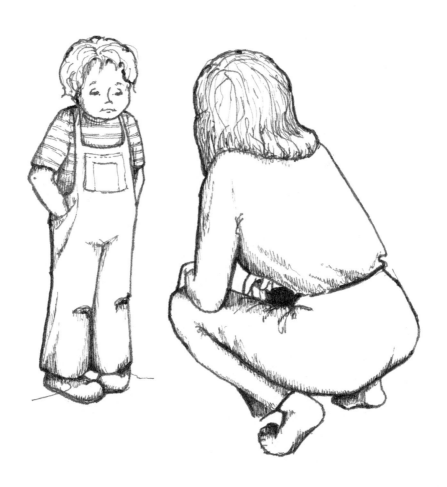

He said he had something for us in his truck.

And did he go get it?

No.

He just left?

No.

Um... Did he say what it was?

Uh-huh.

What?

.... Turkey toes.

Really! I see. And what kind of truck was it?

A great big *giant* truck.

Uh-huh. And what color was it?

What?

The truck!

Purple.

Of course. So then what happened?

The man asked me where to put it.

And what did you tell him?

I told him to put it in the back yard.

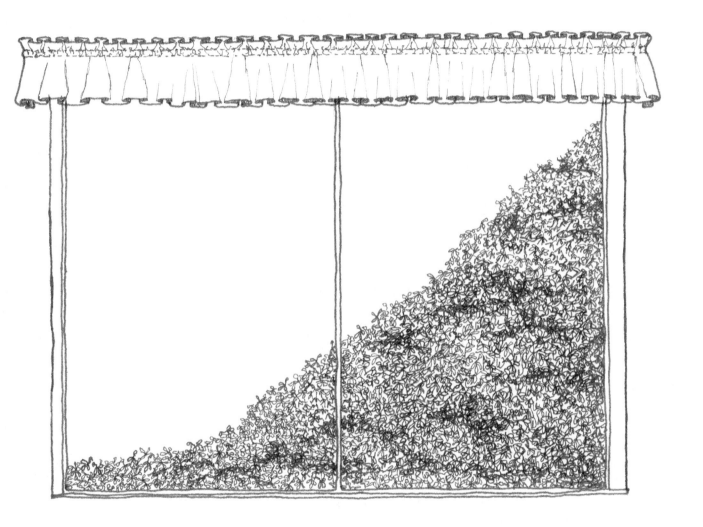

ON BEING A BIRD

I'd like to be a bird.
I could be other things, of course...
An elephant, a cat, a horse,
But I'd rather be a bird.

Why? Well...

Birds can *see* more things.
They fly up high and look around
At all beneath them on the ground.
It's neat when you have wings!

And there's more they can *do*.
They do whatever they're inclined,
Like sitting on a power line
That might shock me and you.

And places they can go...
Why, they can go most anywhere
That you can get to through the air,
And go there *fast*, you know.

A fence won't keep them out.
They don't need tickets to the game,
Don't have to go the way they came.
They're *free* to fly about.

That would be wonderful!
The only thing to be preferred
Would be, I guess, to be a bird
...And be invisible.

MULTIPLICATION

Mindy and Jay were in a field at play
When a tiny parachutist passed their way.
It floated slowly by
In front of Mindy's eye.
"A dandelion tuft," she said to Jay.

"Let's make some more," said Jay, and quickly found
A bushy ball of dandelion down.
And with a mighty puff
He filled the air with fluff --
More parachutists drifting slowly down.

"How many are there?" curious Mindy asked.
"Let's count them," Jay said, kneeling on the grass.
He picked another one,
And then there was begun
The tricky, tiny tuft tallying task.

One hundred ninety-seven was the count
When finally they pulled the last tuft out.
"You know, each one's a seed,"
Said Jay, "and it will be
Another dandelion when it sprouts."

Mindy thought, as then she looked around
Where all the seeds had settled to the ground,
If every seedling bore
Almost two hundred more,
Soon in this field their flowers would abound.

And if **each one** then made two hundred more
It would not be too very long before
They'd fill the neighborhood
And soon the country would
Be dandelion plants from shore to shore.

"And then the world," she thought... but by and by
A puzzled look came into Mindy's eye.
If this were really so,
Would have happened long ago.
"It's **not** all dandelions. I wonder why?"

The two friends talked and rested from their fun
And wondered, as they sat there in the sun,
"Why do these crazy weeds
Make such a lot of seeds
When all each really needs to make is one?"

FISH STORY

This morning I went flying
In a giant flying saucer.
It seems no one believes me, but it's true.
I think 'cause it's a school day
And I was not in school
They figure I just made it up. Do you?

Well, listen, here's what happened.
I was on my way to school
And in that field behind the neighbor's place
When I heard this sort-of humming
And I felt this sort-of heat
And I saw this thing come down from outer space.

It was round and flat and shiny
And bigger than a house...
A real live spaceship. Man, you should have seen 'er!
And then this doorway opened
And it sucked me up inside
Just like a fuzzball in a vacuum cleaner.

Inside it there were creatures
With two heads and three arms
And skin that was a bluish-greyish-green.
At first it was real scary,
But they were nice to me
And showed me things that I had never seen.

They took me up and showed me
What the world looks like from space
Then flew me to the moon and 'round the sun.
And they showed me through their spaceship
With all these weird machines,
Then brought me back to where we had begun.

And then... What? Oh, my pant legs?
How'd they get all wet?
Uh...

They dropped me off just kinda' in the lake.
And this? Oh, yeah, this here...
Well, uh, just as I left
The spacemen gave me this nice fish to take.

A MAGIC SPELL. OR SOMETHING

I used to be rotten at spelling.
It's something I really did hate.
But then I got stung by a spelling bee,
And now I can spell just grate!

STRANGE THINGS TO EAT

Samuel Sesame liked to cook
And almost never used a book
But made up his own dishes, *and*
From anything there was on hand.

Now, you may not think this so strange
Since *lots* of kids are at home on the range;
But when Sam cooked stuff, what appeared
Was... unusual?... no, more like weird.

Like peanut-butter-sliced-grape san',
Cottage cheese with strawberry jam,
Stewed tomatoes, cold, with sugar,
Or a B.L.T. with peanut butter,

Tuna and butter and crunched crackers, fried,
Hot mush with jam or jelly inside,
Cranberry juice and vanilla ice cream,
Or grilled chocolate bar sandwich supreme.

And when friends came to Sammy's place
They'd see his food and make a face
And never even try a bite.
Instead they'd ask, "Are you alright?"

But Sammy didn't really mind;
He'd eat the food that they'd declined,
'Cause what few people understood
Was that the stuff he made... tastes good!

A TUBE FULL OF PEOPLE

Yesterday *I* got to go for a ride
To a place where I never had been;
I went on an airplane up into the sky,
And *I* want to do it again!

To get to the airplane we walked through this place
Like a tunnel. And then I could see
What looked like a bus made to fly into space,
Or a tube full of people to me.

We each got to sit in our own big soft chairs,
And the one by the window was mine.
The window was dinky, but I didn't care,
'Cause when you get close you see fine.

Then we put on these seat belts just like in a car,
And the jet lady told us some things;
And while we were leaving where the parked airplanes are
The jet lady gave me some wings.

Then we drove, no, we **taxied** awhile till we stopped
At the end of a big empty street.
Then the engines got loud and the plane kinda' hopped
And it pushed me back into my seat.

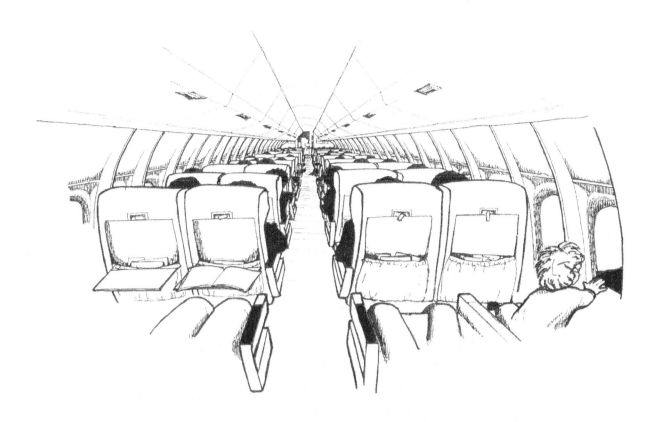

Then I got pushed back harder and harder; it was
… like a rocketship leaving its tower.
But *I* wasn't scared, no, excited because
My dad smiled and said, "Feel the power!"

We went faster and faster and then pretty soon
The whole tube of people tipped back
Like climbing a giant steep hill to the moon
Or a roller coaster climbing its track.

And outside the window the street disappeared
And we were all up in the air
Above all the houses and cars… It was weird!
Why, you could just see everywhere!

We kept going higher and higher, and then
We went right inside of a cloud,
Then out through the top, with the sunshine again
On our wings. Gee, it made me feel proud

To be even higher than birds ever fly
And look down at clouds from above.
And I thought to myself, "Here I am in the sky
Doing something I only *dreamed* of."

Then the jet ladies brought us all something to eat
All arranged on these neat little trays
Which they put on these shelves on the back of each seat.
And the food? Yeah, it tasted OK.

Then we flew and we flew a long time through the air,
And mostly I read and I sat.
One time it got bumpy, but I didn't care
'Cause Dad says planes often do that.

Sometimes you'd feel heavy, sometimes you'd feel light
Like a car on an up-and-down street.
But mostly it was really smooth and just right;
And the hum of the engines was neat.

Then the jet lady said to put on our seat belts
And the airplane began to come down.
Outside it got noisy, and then we all felt
A big bump. We were back on the ground.

It got even *more* noisy and we stopped real fast!
Then we parked by another big jet.
And as we were leaving the jet lady asked
If I liked it, and I said, "You bet!"

GROWNUPS FOR GROWNUPS

I hear and see on TV
And learn about in school
People doin' stuff that's mean and stinkin'.
Like stealin' things, or wars...
The stuff that's really bad
That they should know is wrong. I got to thinkin'...

If Sis and I start fightin'
Our mom 'n dad will stop us
And make us work it out another way.
When Pete took Joey's football
His dad made him return it
And 'pologize to Joey right away.

I guess that what the world needs
Is grownups for the grownups,
Someone calm and wise who won't get mad,
Someone who is patient
And knows just what to do
To stop the grownups from bein' bad.

They'd have to be real powerful
And also super smart
So they could put a stop to wars 'n stuff.
'Cause when whole countries argue
And fight with one another
To break it up takes someone really tough.

I think that we need someone
To come from outer space,
Someone even more grown-up than grownups,
To say, "Shame on you! Stop that!"
And make sure that we all
Behave ourselves until we *really* grow up.

IF I COULD DRIVE A CAR

If I could drive a car,

I'd drive all around my neighborhood and wave at all my friends. Boy would *they* be surprised!

Or I'd find somebody I know who's riding their bike and come up beside them and honk, then I'd zoom on down the street.

Then I'd go find a big empty parking lot and do zig-zags and figure eights frontwards and backwards and stop and go as quickly as I could.

I'd go find a road where there aren't any stoplights, but where there are lots of turns and ups and downs and drive fast, but not so fast that it's scary.

I'd pick a spot way off in the distance, as far as I could see, like the top of a big hill, and just keep driving until I got there.

Then I'd go to my grandparents' house all by myself (I know the way) and pull into their driveway and honk the horn. Boy, would they be surprised!

Oh, but if I could fly an airplane,

I'd take off with a roar and fly high up into the air, then fly up and down and upside down and every way the plane would turn, any way I wanted to go, completely free.

Then I'd go find some birds flying and sneak up on them from behind. (Yikes, where did **he** come from?)

Then I'd fly over my own house and see what's in all the places in my neighborhood you can't see into from the ground, like Mrs. Freibisher's back yard.

I'd fly real low over my school and startle all the teachers... No, I'd wait until recess, then fly over and waggle my wings, then the next day I'd say, "Guess who **that** was."

I'd go find a river and fly real low and turn whenever it turned and keep going until I found where it came from.

I'd fly to the mountains and zip along right down in the deep valleys, then climb up and circle a mountain top, then fly right over it so my wheels almost touched.

Then I'd go find a cloud and blast right through it... and then...

Or if I could run a train,

I'd blow the whistle and start and stop, then I'd... I'd...

Hmmmm.

I think I'll go ride my bike.

GOOD ADVICE

"If at first you don't succeed…"
My father says to me.
"But wait." I say, "Don't tell me 'bout
How stubborn I should be.
It's just that I can't suck these darn
Bananas through my straw.
My milkshake's going to sit and melt."
My father just says, "Aaaw,"
And trades me for his chocolate shake,
And then to me he tells,
"If at first you don't succeed,
Then suck something else!"

HOW TO SKIN AN ELEPHANT

Lets say today, while out at play
You shot an elephant.
Not a kindly one from a circus, say,
But one you're **supposed** to hunt.

So there you are with this big dead thing
Ten times as big as a horse;
And what in the world do you do with it?
Well you **skin** it, of course.

And how do you skin an animal
Whose hide is as tough as a board?
Well the first thing you do is go back home
And get an extension cord...

And some ropes or some chains (and a hat, 'case it rains)
And a winch to attach to a tree
And thirty or forty big, strong plastic bags
And some tape (to connect them, you see)...

And some lumber for braces for hard-to-reach places
And a ladder to climb up on top
And be sure to remember an electric can opener
And perhaps, if you're neat, bring a mop.

So what do you do now with all of this gear
And this beast that you managed to nail?
Well...
You plug in the cord and the electric can opener

and simply

start in

at the tail.

FORTS

Did you ever build a fort?
It's really fun to do.
They're kinda' like a hiding place
Or maybe like a safety place
Just for your friends and you.

You can build 'em in the ground --
A foxhole you can share.
You dig a hole just deep enough
And cover it with brush and stuff
So no one knows it's there.

Or build one in a tree.
You need a tree that's high,
With branches that spread out real good.
You nail on boards and scraps of wood
And hide up there and spy.

Or even at your house,
If there are bushes near,
You make a clearing in the center
And secret passageway to enter
Through which you disappear.

But in my room's a fort
More safe than all the others,
'Cause when I go to bed, you see,
I take a flashlight in with me
And hide beneath the covers.

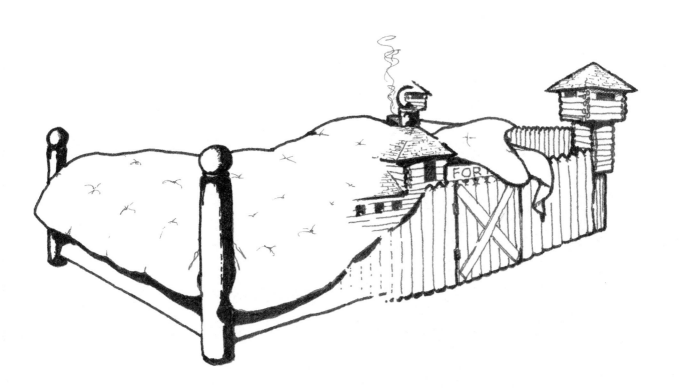

PRETTY CLEVER FOR A RABBIT

While Tim was at play in the woods one day
He turned into a rabbit.
He had no idea what caused him to change;
Just *poof*, and he had had it.
No longer a boy, he was covered with fur
And complete with big rabbit ears
And everything else that a rabbit has.
Why, even his clothes disappeared.

At first he just thought, "It's a dream. So, let's see,
The next thing I'll be is a mouse."
But a rabbit he stayed; so after awhile
He headed on back to his house.
He walked... No, he hopped through the woods to his house
And right on up to his back door.
But then he just stopped; Tim, the rabbit, you see,
Could not reach the knob anymore.

And that's when it hit him and he realized
Just what kind of problem he had.
"I look like a rabbit, so how do I prove
That I'm Timmy to my mom and dad?
If Mom sees a rabbit she'll probably chase me
Back into the woods with her broom.
And Dad, why, he might even go get his gun,
And if I'm still here... boom!"

So quickly he scampered back into the woods
And hid there to think up a plan.
But it wasn't easy, 'cause when you're a rabbit
Just how do you act like a man?
A rabbit can't talk, so you *can't* just go up to
A person and say, "This is me."
And no matter how you might wiggle or wag,
A rabbit is all that they'll see.

So Tim had a problem; and while he was thinking
His dinner time came and it went.
And naturally Timothy's mother and father
Began to get somewhat upset.
So after awhile they both went to the door and
They called, "Timmy, come home and eat."
But Tim didn't answer, and that's when they noticed
A rather strange sight at their feet.

A bunch of small toys that had been in the playhouse
Were there in a line on the ground.
First at the back door, then about every step
Another small toy could be found.
They seemed to be saying to Timothy's parents,
"Come, follow us. Take a walk."
So that's what they did, 'round the house, 'cross the yard,
Until they came to the sandbox.

That's where the line stopped, and so did Tim's parents,
Surprised by what they now looked at,
'Cause there in the sandbox, almost like he owned it,
A very bold rabbit just sat.
But even more strange was that there in the sand
Were written the words, **I AM TIM**
And also an arrow; and that's where the rabbit
Now sat, so it pointed at him.

Then Timothy's father asked, not really serious,
"Timmy, is that really you?"
And when the bold rabbit then nodded his head
Their astonishment naturally grew.
And next Tim's dad asked, "If it's you, how'd it happen?"
And both watched the rabbit then go
To where there was still a clear patch in the sand
And write with his paw,
I DONT NO.

"It has to be Timmy, Dear. Look at his spelling,"
Said Mother, no longer in doubt.
But when she turned quickly and ran for the house
Tim's dad thought, "She's going to freak out!"
He hollered, "Don't worry, Dear, things will be all right.
Please, Dear, be calm, keep your head.
He's a nice looking rabbit, Dear… Where are you going?"
"To the store to buy carrots," she said.

THE FIRST TIME

Did you ever
    wonder how
        some things ever
            came to be
                when at one time
                    no one knew
                        that they could be done?

Take, for instance,
    riding bikes.
        Think how hard
            it was to learn.
                Who'd have guessed
                    it could be
                        so easy and so fun?

Freddy takes
    the violin.
        (Really, he sounds
            terrible!)
                Who first practiced
                    years and years
                        to make one sound so sweet?

Or to tame
    fierce animals...
        that takes patience,
            lots of guts.
                Who first learned
                    it's possible
                        to perform that feat?

Fire... How'd
    the cavemen know
        that if they would
            rub two sticks
                and rub and rub
                    for long enough
                        a fire could be begun?

Engines... Dad says
    so they'll run
        lots of things
            must be just right.
                How did someone
                    ever get
                        the first engine to run?

Some things **sound**
    impossible.
        Maybe some
            we've just not thought of.
                Trick, it seems,
                    is being first
                        to get *around* to them.

Doesn't it
    make you wonder
        how many more
            amazing things
                we'd be doing
                    if we only
                        knew that we could do them?

MY FAVORITE TREE

I have a favorite tree.
It's where I like to be.
I climb up to a branch and sit
Where nobody can see.

And when someone comes by
I stay real still and spy.
It's fun to think that they don't know
I'm watching from up high.

Or sometimes I've preferred
To squawk like some big bird.
They crane their necks and squint their eyes
And wonder what they've heard.

But my most favorite joke's
To drop *apples* on folks.
It drives them nuts because, you see,
My favorite tree's an oak.

THE DRUMMER

I want to learn to play the drum,
Brrrum   pum   pum   pum.
I know I'll be a "hit" at that,
Rat-a   tat   tat   tat.
You'll see how quickly I learn how,
Ti-ti-ti   crash   bam   pow.
Because I really have the knack,
Chink-a   chink-a   boom boom   whack.
Like rick-a-ta   bonk   rick-a-ta   bump.
Ram bam   tap-a tap-a   bang bang   whump.
Boom chick-a   boom chick-a   tiddle diddle   bop.
Thud bump-a   bam bam   clicky ticky   pop.
Boom-a-la-ma   smack-a-whack   boom-a-la-ma   bash,
Tickety lickety   tackity lackity   tockity lockity   crash.
Knock sock-a   p ...
Oh...   uh...

So I'm going to learn to play the drum,
Brrrum   pum   pum   pum.
It's really going to be my thing,

Tink   tink-a   tink   tink-a

tink tink ching.

WHAT DO ANIMALS THINK?

What do animals think, do you think?
How about pets, like a dog or a cat...
What's in their minds when they look up at you
And seem to be saying, "Hey, let's have a chat" ?

Do they understand what you say, would you say?
Do they think in words even though they can't talk?
Or do they just know certain sounds, like their name,
Or "come" or "play dead"; other words are just squawk?

There *are some* things animals know, as you know
Like when it's the time that they normally eat.
But do they consider things... think about stuff,
Like hoping you're going to give them a treat?

Do cats or dogs ever wonder, I wonder.
What goes through their heads while they're still, but awake?
Are they thinking things over? Making some plans?
Do *they* know that they have decisions to make?

Does a dog or a cat really think, do you think?
When a dog takes a swim does it think about sinking?
Or a cat, when it sleeps, does it dream about mice?
And... do they wonder about what *you're* thinking?

THE DATE

Nate took Kate out on a date
And brought her home at half-past eight,
Which wasn't late and wouldn't rate
The scolding that her dad gave Nate
Before he kicked him through the gate
And used some words I can't relate.

The reason? Not the time but date,
'Cause Nate brought Kate back one day late.

I WANT TO BE A GARBAGE MAN

I want to be a garbage man
And drive a big ol' garbage truck
And empty people's garbage cans
And take away their trash and gluck.

It's not the only job that's good;
There's other things that I could be.
But as a garbage man I would
Be **pampered** by my family.

I'd come home from my garbage route;
They'd bring my slippers, feed me chow
And never ask me to take out
The garbage, like I'm doing now.

USED CANDY

I used to have some gum.
I wonder what I did with it?
Oh, yeah, it's stuck here where I sit.
I'll chew it su'more. Yum!

Now, where's my peppermint?
I was suckin' it not long ago.
Oh here, it's in my pocket, though
I'll hafta' lick off the lint.

And here's my candy bar!
It's crumbled into tiny bits
Inside my pocket. Eatin' it
Is gonna be kinda' hard.

Oh, yeah, my choc'lit rabbit…
It's over there, squashed on the floor.
I'll leave *that* so some other poor,
Hungry kid can have it.

TOYS

"Daddy," you said to me,
"I don't want to grow up.
I want to stay little and play and have fun.
I don't *want* to grow up."

"But, honey," I said to you,
"Grownups have fun, too.
The play doesn't stop just because you grow up;
There are always fun things to do."

"But, Daddy," you said to me,
"Grownups don't have any toys.
They don't play with dollies and monsters and stuff
When they're no longer girls and boys."

I said, "That's not quite true.
'Cause I have *my* toys, too.
Like my fishing gear and my stereo,
My golf clubs and canoe."

"See, there are *lots* of things
Grownups get pleasure from.
But of all of the things that there are to enjoy,
My favorite toy is your mom."

LOLLIPOPS AND LEARNING TO FLY

Kid: (to pilot) Hi.
Pilot: Hi there.
Kid: Want a lollipop?
Pilot: No thanks.
Kid: I have a brand new one you can have...
Pilot: No thanks. Lollipops are for kids.
Kid: Don't you like lollipops?
Pilot: Kid, you don't ask a grownup, especially a pilot, if he wants a lollipop.
Kid: Oh. But I just...
Pilot: Look, uh... What's your name?
Kid: Jamie.
Pilot: Look, Jamie, grownups don't eat lollipops, just like kids don't do things like... uh... like fly airplanes. Flying airplanes is for grownups.
Jamie: (sadly) Oh.
Pilot: Um... Listen, let's go over there where we can talk.

Pilot:	Now, Jamie, you want to know a secret? I *like* lollipops, even though I'm a grownup. I just can't let all these other grownups know. They'd think I'm silly. But I'll bet they like lollipops, too.
Jamie:	Yeah, and I'd like to learn to fly an airplane.
Pilot:	Oh, but kids can't... Hmm...
Jamie:	Kids can't fly airplanes?
Pilot:	Sure they can! Jamie, I have a little airplane of my own Would you like to come fly it with me sometime?
Jamie:	Wow, yeah!
Pilot:	Just one thing... You'll have to be sure to bring along an extra lollipop for me.

SOMETHING LEFT TO DO

Someone wrote a poem
But they weren't quite through.
They left out the rhyme;
Now the rhymer's you .

Bessie is a cow
And a cow says ____.
Muffie is a kitten
and a kitten says ____.

Owl up in a tree
And the owl says ____.
People feed the pigeons
And the pigeons say ____.

Happy little baby
With a gurgle and ____.
Rootin' tootin' cowboy
Hollers out ____.

Scary, sneaky ghost
From behind says ____.
Witch is in her kitchen
With a pot of ____.

Jake is a detective
And he needs a ____.
Robert is a cobbler
And he mends a ____.

Tony tends the animals
And he runs a ____.
Jimmy is a chimney sweep
And he cleans a ____.

Don't step on a slug
'Cause a slug makes ____.
Don't inhale the pepper
Or you'll go ____.

Sister skinned her knee;
Now she cries ____.
Brother found a skunk;
Now we all say ____.

LIFE IN A DUNGEON

I live in a dungeon. It ain't all that bad.
The food ain't the greatest that *I* ever had,
And as for the furnishings, they're kinda' plain.
It's cold and it's damp here, but *I* can't complain.

They feed ya real regular - one time a day.
It's always just swill, but what can I say...
At least it ain't spinach or liver or beets,
And if I don't wanna I don't gotta eat.

My bed is a plank. Though it's hard I can take it.
At least in the morning I don't gotta make it.
And morning? It's dark here so how do ya tell?
Easy. My guard comes and lets out a yell.

There ain't much ta do here. It gets kinda boring,
But 'least I ain't gotta go ta work in the morning.
It's really quite peaceful. They leave ya ta think.
Like, lately I'm thinkin' I'm startin' ta stink.

Oh, baths... Yeah, they make ya go wash every week.
But ya don't gotta get ya so clean that ya squeek.
And clothes... Naw, they don't give a darn what ya wear.
I don't wear no tie and I don't comb my hair.

I don't pay no taxes. I don't pay no bills.
I don't see no dentist. I don't take no pills.
I don't do no nuttin' I don't wanna do.
Well, 'cept when the guard makes me polish his shoes.

When things get too boring I try ta escape.
They beat me then but, hey, it keeps me in shape.
And what with my diet I never get fat.
And sun-damaged hair? Naw. Hey, pale's where it's at.

Variety? Well yeah, sure, I get my share,
Like when I'm chained up to the wall over there.
Sometimes right side up and sometimes upside down.
There's all sorts of ways for just hangin' around.

So ya' see, in this joint life ain't really half bad.
A dungeon's a heckuva lazy man's pad!
When it comes to the easy life I've got it made.
'Course, life on the outside ain't bad. Wanna trade?

THE MARCHING BAND

Us kids in the neighborhood, we used to have a band.
It wasn't very fancy, just us kids, you understand.

But, really, there were uniforms and instruments we made.
We picked some tunes and practiced, and we really marched and played.

We didn't have real instruments, so we had to invent 'em
Except Jim's army bugle that an uncle once had sent him.

Our cymbal girl banged saucepan lids (and plugged her ears with gum),
And one kid brought a garbage can and that was our bass drum.

Another of our drummers played by banging two wood blocks;
And one guy took a metal pipe and hit it with a rock.

One kid had a whistle and an air-horn that he blew;
Another rang a cowbel and the rest all played kazoo.

Our uniforms were T-shirts, jeans, and yellow baseball caps
(Which kinda' matched our drum major who waived a baseball bat.)

We practiced in the playfield and we marched real straight and proud.
We didn't really sound so good, but man, we sure were loud!

In fact, our band was loud enough that people used to say
That they could hear us playing six or seven blocks away!

We marched right up and down the street once we had got the knack.
And once we marched through Jim's front door (Jim's mom ran out the back).

That band was sure a lot of fun; it kept us *on* the street
(Although our parents didn't seem to think it was that neat).

Our neighborhood is quiet now; there have been no more bands.
It seems ours died the day our parents gave us all Walkmans.

THE KID WHO LIVES UPSTAIRS

There is a kid who lives upstairs
And spends most of his time inside;
He won't come out much anymore,
But seems to want to hide.

I don't recall when he moved in,
And he's been shy for quite awhile.
It's strange, 'cause he's the kind of kid
Makes other people smile.

And on those times he **does** come out
It's usually to laugh and play.
He's much more skilled at having fun
Than me, I'd have to say.

But when I **want** him to emerge
That's very rarely what he'll do.
Yet there are times he'll show up when
I least expect him to.

It isn't often he'll appear
In stuffy grown-up company;
But he'll come out with kids around,
Or when it's only me.

And sometimes he'll surprise me with
A wild and crazy thing or two
That dignified adults like me
Just wouldn't *dare* to do.

I really think I envy him;
Though shy, he's also wild and free,
So able to amuse my friends
And make a fool of me.

Some people think I should evict
This crazy kid from my upstairs.
He *can* embarrass me, and yet
I'm rather glad he's there.

ABOUT THE AUTHOR

Reid Brockway is a retired electrical engineer / systems analyst living part-time in Sammamish, Washington, and part-time in eastern Washington along Lake Entiat, a dammed-up portion of the Columbia River, a place he refers to as, "The Liver".

Made in the USA
Las Vegas, NV
16 June 2021